"The tesseraic language of Tongo Eisen-Martin's *Heaven Is All Goodbyes* brings a new, shared articulation to the intricacies and interconnections of grief and life, speech and site, state and inhabitant, violence and landscape. Here, polyvocal assemblages gather and revolt against our 'porcelain epoch / succeeding for the most part / dying for the most part / married for the most part to its death.' This is resistance as sound."—**CLAUDIA RANKINE**

"I don't know that there is a living writer whose work loves Black people as much as Tongo Eisen-Martin's work loves us. In *Heaven Is All Goodbyes*, like all of Eisen-Martin's work, this Black love is not clumsy, easy, sentimental or reliant on spectacle. That Black love lives in the cracked history and ambient future of who we've been in the dark, and what's been done to us in the light. These poems somehow watch and listen without intervening. And when they ask, they ask everything. *Heaven Is All Goodbyes* makes me want to live, and write, with us forever."—**KIESE LAYMON**, author of *Long Division*

"What a wonderful feeling for life. If we are born—we will die. If we love—we will be rejected. If we are rejected—we will leave. The balance of these poems, one against another, gives us laughter, love and hope. Heaven *isn't* goodbye—it's only the next stop on our heart's journey."—**NIKKI GIOVANNI**

"Yet again Tongo Eisen-Martin employs his blade-sharp intellect, his wry and piercing wit and unflinching candor to make poems that matter. This collection demands that the reader see[s ...] than themselves—both on the page a[nd ...] The poems beg to be read aloud, to [...]

incantations, as reports back from communities both known and shrouded. Read this work. Then read it again. Again. Again."
—CHINAKA HODGE, author of *Dated Emcees*

"This striking new work from Tongo Eisen-Martin is a timely reminder of Amiri Baraka's call for poems that are *useful*, poems that breathe like wrestlers. At every turn, *Heaven Is All Goodbyes* demands that we engage the systemic violence woven into our daily living right alongside the persistent force that is black social life, the joy that everyday people cultivate against unthinkable odds. And even though Eisen-Martin grounds us, necessarily, in the material constraints of the modern world, he doesn't leave us there. He calls us elsewhere. He brings us with him into a robust, illuminating vision of the worlds that exist outside and underneath the one that seeks to curtail our liberation, contain our love. This is work that challenges as it lifts. These are the unabashed abolitionist lyrics of a writer who knows that stakes are high and so is the cost of conceding our most radical dreams. In a moment marked by cynicism and disenchantment, Eisen-Martin remains a believer: in the commons, in collective struggle, in our capacity to flourish in the midst of what we were never meant to survive."
—JOSHUA BENNETT, author of *The Sobbing School*

HEAVEN IS ALL GOODBYES

Tongo Eisen-Martin

Pocket Poets Series : Number 61
City Lights Books | San Francisco

Cover art: Biko Eisen-Martin

Library of Congress Cataloging-in-Publication Data

Names: Eisen-Martin, Tongo, author.
Title: Heaven is all goodbyes / Tongo Eisen-Martin.
Description: San Francisco : City Lights Publishers, [2017] |
Series: City lights pocket poets series ; 61
Identifiers: LCCN 2017017696 | ISBN 9780872867451
  (softcover)
Subjects: LCSH: African Americans--Poetry | BISAC: POETRY /
  American / African American.
Classification: LCC PS3605.I8275 A6 2017 | DDC 811/.6--dc23
LC record available at https://lccn.loc.gov/2017017696

ISBN: 978-0-87286-745-1

City Lights books are published at the City Lights Bookstore
261 Columbus Avenue, San Francisco, CA 94133.
www.citylights.com

CONTENTS

The dedication:

Like 50 familiar postures in the dark ... Run here. We will save your life.

Faceless

A tour guide through your robbery
He also is

Cigarette saying, "look what I did about your silence."

Ransom water and box spring gold
        —This decade is only for accent grooming, I guess

Ransom water and box spring gold
        —The corner store must die

War games, I guess

All these tongues rummage junk

                The start of mass destruction
                      Begins and ends
                   In restaurant bathrooms
                    That some people use
               And other people clean

      "you telling me there's a rag in the sky?"
               —waiting for you. yes—

we've written a scene
we've set a stage

We should have fit in. Warehouse jobs are for communists. But now more corridor and hallway have walked into our lives. Now the whistling is less playful and the barbed wire is overcrowded too.

My dear, if it is not a city, it is a prison.
If it has a prison, it is a prison. Not a city.

When a courtyard talks on behalf of military issue,
all walks take place outside of the body.

Dear life to your left
Medieval painting to your right
None of this makes an impression

Crop people living in thin air
You got five minutes
to learn how to see
through this breeze

When a mask goes sideways,
Barbed wire becomes the floor
Barbed wire becomes the roof
Forty feet into the sky
becomes out of bounds

When a mask breaks in half,
mind which way the eyes go.

They've killed the world for the sake of giving everyone the
same backstory

We're watching Gary, Indiana fight itself into the sky

Old pennies for wind. For that wind feeling you get before the hood goes up and over your headache. Pennies that stick together (mocking all aspirations). Stuck together pennies was the first newspaper I ever read. Along with the storefront dwelling army that always lets us down.

Where the holy spirit favors the backroom. Souls in a situation that offer one hundred ways to remain a loser. Souls watching the clock hoping that eyes don't lie to sad people.

> *"what were we talking about again?"*
> *the narrator asked the graveyard*
> *—ten minutes flat—*
> *said the graveyard*
> *—the funeral only took ten minutes—*
> *"never tell that to anyone again,"*
> *the narrator severely replied*

"You just going to pin the 90s on me?"
—all thirty years of them—
"Then why should I know the difference between sleep and satire?"

the pyramid of corner stores fell on our heads
—we died right away

that building wants to climb up and jump off another building
—these are downtown decisions

somewhere on this planet, it is august 7th

and we're running down the rust thinking, "one more needs to
    come with me"

"What
evaporated
on earth, so
that we could
be sent back
down?"

A conductor of minds
        In a city-wide symphony
        Waving souls to sing
        He also is

The Course of Meal

Apparently, too much of San Francisco was not there in the first place

This dream requires more condemned Africans
Or (put another way)
State violence rises down
Or
Still life is just getting warmed up
Or
Army life is looking for a new church and ignored all other suggestions
Or
Folk tale writers have not made up their minds as to who are going to
    be their friends

"this is the worst downtown yet. And I've borrowed a cigarette
    everywhere
. . . I've taken many a walk to the back of a bus that led on out
    the back of a
storyteller's prison sentence, then on out the back of slave scars."

"Though this is my comeback face."

"I left my watch on the public bathroom sink and took the toilet
with me. I threw it at the first bus I saw eating single mothers half
alive. It flew through the bus line number, then on out the front of
the white house"

hopefully you find comfort downtown. But if not, we've brought you
enough cigarette filters to make a decent winter coat

a special species of handshake
lets all know who's king and what the lifespan is of uniform cloth

> *this coffin needs to quit acting like those are birds singing*
> *rusty nails have no wings*
> *have no voice other than that of a white world dying*
> *there are book pages in the gas pump*
> *catchy isn't it?*
> *the way three nooses is the rule*
> *or the way potato sack masks go well with radio codes*

Or the way condemned Africans fought their way back to the
   ocean only to find waves made of
1920s burned up piano parts
European backdoor deals
            and red flowers for widows who spend all day in the
      sun mumbling at San Francisco

"red flowers, but what's the color of a doctor visit?"

There are book titles in the street

Book titles like:

Hero, You'd Make A Better Zero

Fur Coat Lady, The President Is Dead

Pay Me Back In Children

They Hung Up Their Bodies In Their Own Museums

—and other book titles pulled out of a drum solo

RUN HERE, HERO!
—lied the hiding place

all the bullets in ten precincts know where to go
there's no heaven (nor any other good ideas) in the sky
politics means: people did it and people do it.
understand that when in San Francisco
and other places that were never really there

bet this ocean thinks it's an ocean
but it's not.
it's just 6th and mission street.

"All know who is king. King of thin things. Like america. I'm
proud to deserve to die ... I will eat my dinner extra slow
tonight in this
police state candy dispenser that
you all call a neighborhood ... "

no set of manners
goes unpunished
never mind about
a murderer's insomnia
or the tea kettle preparing everyone for police sirens

I have to talk to myself differently now

When a drummer is present,
They are God

"I am not an I.
I am a black commons"

        I am writing out my new tattoo on bus station glass
                making tattoos all afternoon
          talking myself into seeing the decade through

           under my skin, they call a tattoo the sky

          I must really be the devil's front man

          staring at an empty bus that I imagine,
             in fact, carries paintings of people

     and the man drunk behind the wheel
        has to choose between
        a black and white toddler
        afterschool in america
        on a california street
        that doesn't need a name
        nor a california

     no one on the street has a job
        and therefore
        no one is there

"I colored my oppressor's gun
and dance floor for him in the same day,"
the joke began

"the walk under bus seats is fine by me
as long as I get to the front,"
the joke concluded

and Tuesday is a
rotten soup
or downhill
entertainment
or commotion in the
ashtray
or the day jail quotas
get filled
the day that the
planet plays flat

Maybe the capitalist
sets stadium seats
on fire
and calls it economic
progress

The communist has plenty of time
To finish his cigarette
and lie to his boss

A killer lying down in front of a tank
I have a small statue built in my chest
and also, an anchor upside down in the air

worried about the walls
I forgot the ceiling was closing in on me too
—my take on my alcoholism

I am hunched over a meal
I ate five years ago
—my take on the look on my face

                    He cursed God a little
              then took another step up the staircase

        and for a second, forgot all occupants of the world
                              beginning with this house

he (this action hero of one street proportions) declared:

"rap music is the way I count blessings. The '80s were better than
its fiction. I got a piece of fence meshed through my skull. I will
be half-eaten my entire life. Always walking beside myself with a
gun to my head and another one pointed at passers by. And it's
half of me or all of you. Walking in and out of myself. But I'm
always happy to see you, brother. What a miraculous route you
took through the threat!"

honest pay
is a knife in his arm

honest pay in my chest
is a broken lock on the monument

tell you the truth
I forget what his hands looked like
What he did with them
What kind of third eye the cuffs cut into his wrist

The Confidence Scheme

The neighborhood looks like someone put their kitchen outside /
    Like our children love Detroit / And therefore it is better to cry
    than cry through your hands

(I've been rehearsing my speeches all summer / tracing car keys on
    paper and calling it poetry)

I'm reaching
through the chair
Into the back of a rib cage   (the metaphor is the chair)

I am a spirit who sketches
        And thinks too much for a man killed by a herd

                A poor man's coat becomes my leader
                But will soon need a decent eulogy

                Waiting for a bus station to become
more like a birthday eve than juvenile jail sentence
                is a matter of contraband.

"I will buy you a drink tomorrow,"
        the pain here told the pain there

Wave At The People Walking Upside Down

I am off to make a church bell out of a bank window

> "kitchens meant
> more to the masses
> back in the day"

> and before that?

> "we had no enemy"

somewhere in america
the prison bus is running on time

you are going to want
to lose that job
before the revolution hits

> *Somewhere I won't be home for breakfast.*
> *Everyone out here now knows my name.*
> *And I won't be turned against for at least four months.*

The cop in the picket line is a hard working rookie.
The sign in my hand is getting more and more laughs
It says, "the picket line got cops in it."

> "I can take care of
> those windows for you if you want,

but someone else
has to go in your gas tank"

was clear to the man that
rich people had talked too much this year

go ahead and throw down that marble park bench
everyone is looking up at,
you know,
get the Romans out of your mind

Maybe a good night's sleep
would have changed
The last twenty years of my life

—Playing an instrument
Is like punching a wall—

What would you have me do?
Replace the population?
Give brotherhood back to the winter?
Stop smoking cigarettes with the barely dead?

They listen in on the Sabbath

Police called the police on me
—a white candlestick beneath my detention

"I've ruined the soup again,"
thought the judge

as he took off his pilgrim robe
behind a white people's door (and more)

"I didn't get lucky. I got
what was coming to me,"
he toasts

"fight me back,"
the man said, of course, to himself

washing windows with a will to live
tin can on his left shoulder
enjoying the bright brand new blight
with all partygoers
(both supernatural and supernaturally down to earth)

what, is this elevator traveling side to side?

Like one thousand bitter polaroid pictures that you actually try to eat
All the furniture on this street is nailed to the cement
Cheap furniture, but we have commitment

This morning, an essay opens the conversation between enemies
"why, because you control every gram of processed sugar
between here and a poor man's border?"
"because in the tin can on my left shoulder
I can hear the engines of deindustrialization?"

—You should get into painting,
You know,
Tell lies more deeply—

This month, I'm rooting for the traitor

Carting cement to my pillow ... "here we will build"

                    I am high again. Not talking much.

          Climb the organ pipe up to our apartment floor

               I'm high again. Calling everything church.
                         Singing along to the courtyard.

                    Thanks to a horn player's holy past time

                         Climb up to the rustiest nail

          —Put a real jacket on it
          Talk about a real five years—

Keep memories like these
In my pocket
Next to the toll receipt

That man lost a wager
with the god of good causes,
you know,
stood up for himself
a little too late
(maybe too early)

I can still see
Twenty angles of his jaw
Zigzagging through
The cold world
Of deindustrialization

"there's an art to it," I will tell my closest friends one day

The Simplicity of Talent

The first cigarette makes this parking lot my bedside

The second cigarette makes this parking lot my front pocket

Next I hold the witness like a newborn ... though halfhearted

Brittle teeth by my art,
watch how we talk in depopulated circles

     "you caught me," said the hangman to the condemned
   "caught me red handed," but the hangman's hand kept moving
     nevertheless

biting flags east bound and
other familiar sound effects
—a revolutionary would call us a landless fire

the night train agrees that these are my keys

          "I'm just admiring your fabric, Lord"

my art is rational
therefore my life is in danger

traveling back up the tap this time
and it looks like water was never here
just jail noise
and the jail noise that politicians speak

"the world is weak, brother ... lost its graffiti too many times."

I tell the witness that all characters are in motion regardless of what
    that day did to your disposition

"I also left that piece of good news in the ashtray next to my
    nickname"

Every room has a kitchen in it
Every life has company to feed
Every room has a rumble in the corner

8th grade heroin in my hand
                        pieces of an uncle

    a purgatory grease fire got us worried

a phone rings in 1988
and an epoch begins after a mother hangs up

                        This is not writing poems
                        This is wishing carloads well

Heaven Is All Goodbyes

A 1978 statement

My brother Biko and I are driving
In an empty cell lane

We are God's evil to these settlers
They might throw us under the shift change

We take wolf naps

We don't know what else we good at besides this traveling

State lines in a night tide passing through beachhead america
Passing with hurricane memory
—Three thousand exits of sludge-bathed apartheid

Everything south of canada is extrajudicial gun oil
And your local unemployment factory

In a few hours we will fit in   Relax for now

Hop out of the car and I'm a dirty shoe illusion
Leaning on the trunk with the ghosts of switchblades
                                        And other rusty services

I am enemy humor
And traveling

Father's ashes on the back seat behind two sons

                                        In a lane not for metaphor
                    Well, maybe a metaphor about something unfinished
                    —One million hands passing us through the Midwest

Last wishes by way of fishtail / Day dreams by way of collision /
    Home in the badlands of translation / Relaxed passing / Great
    grandparents' finger bones / Father's ashes / No longer arms /
    Just tattoos

Badlands imagination
Barreling
Translating
A father's last trip home

We don't know what else we good at besides this traveling

Exits in collage / Exits in pieces / Pieces of 1970s kitchen plates /
    In a good luck refrigerator / We still ain't ate / The narcotic
    swing of how we see yesterday

Get out of the car against desperate white supremacy

Gas station greetings
Stray dogs
And other earth-born alarms
        We are stray deadly

Against desperate white supremacy / And other senses /
    That die silly / And have murdered

We don't know what else we good at
Besides this traveling

Two coins / or the toll is us

Character interstate on a journey of a million parallels

Some like us better high / Some like us better drunk / Every late
    night has a summer to it / Cousin breeze and murder rate

Barreling like gut born love songs
Your ancestors are smiling
As we pass the time
When we ride
It's language

Passed Gary 3000
Cast iron lining / Proud forearms for meals

Three-man ghost story

Fishers of ourselves

Cards dealt

Narrative implied

Maybe something unfinished

Like an Indiana hurricane
Or two midnights in Milwaukee

Or no arms
No tattoos
No Chicago
Ever again

We don't know what else we good at
Besides this traveling

And besides
Heaven is all goodbyes
Anyway

may we all refuse to die at the same time

"I believe I wasn't born yet, when a young woman put her first
    gun under a car seat,"
The painter explained
in front of his work
with a .38 in his back pocket

Combination of conversations you may call it:
The day all the saints clocked in late
mixed with the first serious talk
seven-year-old best friends have about war.

              What war stories taught me I now teach you

                 "the world is just a constellation of walls.
                    Twitch a little less than everyone else.
                          That's the key."

I miss her
Or is the static of a westbound interstate bus ride beautiful when
all but three people are asleep

I'm writing poems for the rest of my life again

Taught by the greats:
       "friends make friends. you just be a good liar."
       "you would not believe the grains of blue I found after I
           was laid to ground."
       "fit in, youngster / fit in, trigger man."

"watch your nickname mean something to more than five
people."

Conversations about how a white giant
born without a third dimension
Is wandering under county jail slippers
and people who smoke by themselves in old city parks

and how

Electric chairs are not complicated:
Have a drink. Go to work.

"They lynched his car too. Strung it up right next to him ...
A smart man makes up his own set of holidays ... A smart
man occasionally switches the dates around of his holidays
too. Because enemies have a sense of humor."

Mind. I had a mind once. Served my immediate family well. But
that's all over now.
Now I live in america

A most impressive reimagining of a painter

Up here
Where the tenth floor
Might as well be a cloud of dust
Or a version of myself that
I can point your attention to
While I count my money and curse mankind

The best way to pay me
Is in my left hand
While my right is juggling
A cigarette
A steering wheel
And a negotiation with the ruling class

Maybe you are not a sleepy employee in a project lobby
Maybe you are blood on a fiber
Maybe you are my friend

I have ruled the world.
Let me sleep this off.
Is that your tongue in the sky?
That's the only weather I need.

Lazy conversation
—the only way physics advances

my right hand jogs away from the band

this getaway is live

this instrument
is not yet invented

Coming down
With the rest of the sound
—the young woman and me about to be born

"And there. There is you. Dancing with someone's daughter in front of the precinct"

Look at this ghost that thinks it can fly

"A bunch of dreams
      you don't want coming true
            become a batch," I said to the woman
                  in the living room

my paint was running like my shadow
had more of me
than I did

"what's the matter with your shirt," she asked

"same thing that's wrong with yours,"
                  I said to myself

"My shadow has more of me than me,"
                  I said next to myself

The way to peace in the city
Can be achieved
On no lower
Than the tenth floor

"you remember the elevator you took up here?"
                  I ask

"this city has more of me than me," she said to herself

. . .

"who turned the lights off on my haircut," interrupts a man

the woman is startled

I start deciding whether
I'm alive or differently alive

If there are details to this man's life,
Only he can see them

The only way to have friends in this city
Is no higher than the 16th floor

"I'm differently alive," I say to myself

I throw the man a book of matches

"where the hell has he been hanging out lately?"
she wonders to herself
she cannot see the man

Skid Bid

Lord, here comes the tap water whistling past our heads

Institution tile under brake pedals
    Matching the white watches
        painted on palms for smash and grab recollections

People who are related by ballad:

    hotplate failures fishing for proletarians

    the matchstick that is a draft card
        (by the time the loner finishes sweeping the train)

Also related by ballad:
    under-paved streets hanging like strips of film in thin air

        Brother, I miss the carpentry more than the religion

I tore the tattoo out of my uncle's picture and lent it to my friends
        one left cross at a time

        —for life mimed behind my back

the child would do better upside down:

the child's cake party is in the precinct / mainstream tune playing
    upside down
        a t-shirt with their face printed on a cop's thumb

twenty-eight hours later, a headrest will do

the city rain feels like clientele
I dozed on the back of a bus and
woke up in the mind of a three-story man

"God wants you here with that crowbar in your hand ... all of the
    world is a third floor."

                                        seasons invent themselves
                                but we invent the underground

—cause and effect is nothing but a casual venue I once played—

he decided not to kill me like giving loose change
don't teeter now, tall man
nobody at point blank
nobody finally again

lung first I fell

a love
then
a rule
then
a hate
                    dance moves within murder attempts within dance moves

"*Lean back and be celebrated by small people,*" he said. The clothes on
my life teacher needed new patches. "*Sit back and disrespect it all*"

39

"I've given up on counterrevolution," I said
"Well then here is your weapon, Little Bank"

—That's our father you are writing graffiti on—

Horn players beat me up
and everyone left the altercation a better person

"knowing what you know now
would you still have written fortunes
on the bottom of church shoes
and put them back on the rack?"

"How does everyone think that a rich guy is their twin?"
—along with other tantrums is my cue

fortune teller half sleeps while talking about a mayor treading all
over the posters in my childhood room and how cold
calculation mothers nothing and a vision of
chess pieces in chains . . .

"Then you will have fear. Then you will have form."

Where Windows Should Be

"How did I miss that brother's name?"
    said the sorriest man in the crowd
    with candlelight on his face

                Someone who looks just like you
                came through earlier
                and said he was the devil
                We stopped him before
                he could crack his first joke

                "I can't wait to fall out the sky
                on these suckers again,"
                he mumbled walking away

                "I guess greetings end
                when the knife gets dull,"
                he also mumbled

every once in a while
blood jumps back into the body
and the cosmos go home
(easygoing art)

a woman stops to steady herself,
but her shoulder keeps walking
a man stops to tie his shoes,
but his tongue keeps walking
an infamous child

meets an infamous street
and pulls off an infamous miracle

a gambler came through earlier
looking just like you

we put his head on a paint brush
and got back to work

arguing with each other:

"what do you mean puddles don't smile?"

"and why can't jail bars un-bloom?"

"we call them crumbs! You call them crumbs!"

arm in arm
back alleys walk
after becoming people

rights, baby! Even we get rights too!

A man plays a trumpet next door
Then never no more

I whispered once
It didn't go well
Wine in my cup
They called it a yell

Don't make a scene
All friendships have dead people in them

"you are the one folding up bottles like paper
and putting them under windshields!"

"it's only weird
when no one else plays along!"

Candlelight on faces
The riot keeps walking

She Would Untitle This

Rooftops were not for chasers
But rather for
a rusty small pistol in her purse
Next to his cigarettes

She made her own dresses
He is not her type
It is never Friday night in her apartment

Sleepy luck
Cigarette sleeping on his lip
A man with no future
Kick drum only
Solo in brick

Love survives the summer

World on a Kite String

After I got the first bump over with,
    the conversation wheezed to life in the space between houses

"sounds like a dance ... mouse and mouse"

the bottle brags
that all of us
are almost empty

somewhere over there is a knife ... pass it to me

"I tell her it is all black and white ... then I pull white out of
black ... Lord, my life is like a tambourine toy ... I intended
to go straight ... I put down all my dogs ... I burned my holy
books ... I flushed pictures of presidents down the motel toilet
... I spent my lucky coin in a strip mall"

"I tell her it is all black and white and what it is like to be loved
while riding on the tale of a serpent that is swallowing itself."

"feel far away don't you?"
—cool thing to say to a robbery witness

in a single sitting, the people ate themselves ... off of broken
dishes ... fingers fumbling fingers ... fingers fumbling teeth ...
the dream transforms among friends ... and so bullets can be
funny.

Then sacred ground gave its sanctity
to the hand of a homeless man,

... I can tell who you think has power ...

these days he sleeps under a roof
and the revolution is in a different city

"Saw a piece of white chalk
that reminded me of a clothes pin"

"they urgently want you
back in the waiting room, sir"
—but that's me on the table—

finally had a father on my deathbed
—my final upbringing—

and faith in my lady's singing voice

signed my last name then bowed

Open air churches and other signs of war crimes.
I'm one of the children when I open the front door.
Watching the ghetto crash land.
Open the car door and I am one of the men.
Old-timer when I load the gun.
Loading the gun when my lady wakes up next to me.

Chew stick for a blank check
Chew stick for a blanket statement

And a cigar can be an ancestor
On the coin side of a kite string

Selling What Slaves Made

Nothing worked in the ring, man.

I took my angel on one
        I mean really divided him from God

They write books backwards about fights like mine

a lone wolf in three pieces
everything we know of duty, we made up

                                Maker, My Maker
            Born in a garbage pile outside of a silver mine
                Garbage pile or pile of alley rugs?

                I think I dealt with your death well, Lord
            Garbage pile or shelf full of inner-city poems?

                  Silver mine or interstate rhymes?

        Looking up at the floor tile
        I learned how to dodge rain on purpose

        Looking up at the floor tile
        I cursed at my secondhand shoes
        I cursed up at my secondhand heaven

Although thankfully, I had no brothers behind the milk crates

Had no father where your cracks make an interesting contortion
    of border
And speed up war stories

Police daydream at me
        While someone's laying puddle-side
                                    Half curled up
                                    Half related to no one

Don't put this on your temple wall
Don't put a temple in the middle of this side room

Don't twitch yourself to death
Don't take yourself so serious that your soul falls off

                                    I'm down on my luck
                                    Making snow angels
                        On the abandoned factory loading dock
                                    Looking up at the
                        Tonsils of a non-African deity

                            We are going to stay right here
                            Until the third world comes

        "a beautiful rejection though"
        —we call Europe distant criminality and toast to it

a ten pound weight on your shoulders can kill you
if applied the american way

straightforward philosophy finds me well
well meaning
                    a flood only means one thing on the west coast

—made to struggle on top of people
the reformist's class contradiction continues in thin air
one of the many phantom skylines collapsing
too bad our gasoline means nothing to their world
because we would certainly lend it—

wise man, if you didn't win the war / we would call you a nobody
and look for advice in other Louisiana houses

                    "well that's a funny way of declaring me a saint"
                        I can be two things to all people . . .
                            Old or a hammer

"the world is this pile of clothes"
"the world is this pile of worlds"
—maybe I'll hang on to my style a little longer

the jailer moonwalks to the switch
"may your skin end up
on a tambourine in the deep south"

                            tendered my death threat
                    on a lounge napkin with three stains

                    talking about biological parenting
                    and the presents I brought to powder

laughing a little
then laughing hard

my empty hand takes a bow
—final impersonation
front row with the sirens

a field
of gun handles
is better than
most fantasies

and
sequence counts
only for survivors

The Mission Turns

Sitting across the dinner table from an imploding father figure.
Men like us make it hard to believe in collective afterlife lately.
Imploding father figures stockpiled (actually).

> mind then hunger then mind

Gang structure and a good God reminds me of being safe within a
door frame.

Thoughts like these don't mind clinging to the curtains, looking
back at you with smirks, asking, "how did you sleep?"

Russian Roulette

Pull.
A mother goes straight to heaven and back
Pull.
Let's raise that boy on a rack

Roses on a bullet—Right hand stopped engraving after that

        Come back and get high off what you think life is

It's eighty-early and the fortuneteller on my left shoulder cannot
    stay focused

             A loose cannon is in charge of the world
          And I have an imagination you would not believe
       I mean, really have no need for floors nor ceilings

—We are on the hard side of fire—
Opposite easy and godless things

                    Headed to war
                with armor made from
                  cast prison letters
                And other clothes
                  that don't fit

Watching people backflip off of a nickel

Cash in a dollar store pot
Along with the fingers of freaks
And soda machine gavels
(all ingredients loosely defined)

—we are on the hard side of fire—
bragging about the guarantee that God lives and is never bored

tall grass—all this talking—
tall grass is all this talk will ever be

same countdown I've lost to my whole life
counting childhood twice

you know, it's tough when an artist doesn't know if Harlem was
real. It's like spending your life under a fake name. Or drinking
wine to wash down a crumbled cork

I used to like shooting dice nonviolently.
That means with no chance of being rich one day.

Will I be a junkie my whole life?

"Probably, grandson
You see, we made too many bones
before you were born
Your father spent too much time in prison
And your mother is not the sane one
Good con runs in your snot
Your skin is old ground where old
beasts know their way around"

Do funerals have bells?

> "No they don't.
> Not the ones that matter anyway.
> You will be unmarked even to God.
> Unmarked for a thousand years then only seen by God."

And what is death?

"Death is a new toy for you to kick
out of windows and
throw off of walls"

Say Harlem

A masterpiece is coming
(It just has to beat a million bullets to the spot)

Pull.
Man, these guns are about as irrelevant
as the house would call the paint

Pull.
A good night's sleep arrives bleeding on the porch.
Proud parents we have.

Pull.
Genocide has a pair of shoes in my closet too

Pull.
We make bones casually. Over here. On the hard side of fire

The Incense Is Me Smiling

I play cards with her still and do not know which one of her dresses
is her favorite. She gives me the end of a thread and says "this is for
us." She gives me the end of another piece of string and says, "this is
for tomorrow if it comes."

How hard is it for any pair of hands to do anything?

> I sleep on the floor every once in a while
> weaponless

> Next morning is me the wolf

> Some parts of the city
> are not for art
> —no sacred
> geometry

"may you swim out of this business alive," she said
and I never thought again about being more than a man

I did right by the imaginary people that an american winter made
real and then I made imaginary again.

I am your historian. If people beat me down to my place, why
should I not make my disagreement with people? If people sell me
what slaves made ...

Greater men than you have died in this kitchen with the same look

that everyone pretends to not see on your face
"yeah, the news might lie. But someone will never forget"

Beat down in the corner of her mind, or maybe I am out of my
car on a bridge. Have a drink with me, traitor ... I know I am
supposed to go outside and do something

                                    ease away from her arm
                        if you have traded places with the needle

Snuck Between Pews Too

1. Not A Psalm

Thinner streets mean somewhere God is tired of this brand of
cigarettes, congregation, and stash

And the dry skin of trembling mouths biting at the world

> *Baby, the smoke is not going to do it for you this time.*
> *You are going to have to kill this God yourself*

Hangman, hangman:
Your word is starting to mean more around here

Go to the bathroom and wash a few hundred hands

> Heaven being
> the first sun up in a
> chain of events

We are quick because you are sleepwalking
We are dead and spirit mostly

We are the people that people don't want to identify with
You know,
The red light porch
The lookalike Saturdays
The unpopular street sign
The old man who waves

Where you find your cousin drinking for three
And one more by sundown the neighbors predict

> The last sundown in
> a chain of events that
> makes you go off to kill God

2. No Psalm In Sight

> *This liquor store's a has-been*
> *But me*
> *I'm just getting started*
> *I've seen stars walk away in disbelief*
> *The real ones*
> *That makes planets possible*
> *Those are my biggest fans*
> *Biggest victims*
>
> *I talk to dollars too*
> *A hundred names*
> *A character talking to a character in my mind*
> *I got paper bags for canvas*
> *Untouched, but canvas nevertheless*
> *And there are still some characters that got to go*
>
> *I kill*
> *I kill when my clothes don't fit right*
> *When I've walked for too long*
> *When this coffee cup offends me*
> *Who do you kill?*
> *Besides yourself every 20 minutes*

Get your throat off that piece of stained glass, chump

There's no way of life around here
We smoke cigarettes and drink coffee across the street from redemption
What did you think we were looking at, chump?
What else could we be looking at like that?
Between canvas and redemption, all type of things
you can do in the middle of a story ...
I mean all kinds of things you can say to a dollar bill

What do you think we are doing out here?

My mother's across the street
I see her as clear as this Saturday morning sketch
My son is across the street
... My trumpet part is on this paper bag ...
... Another star walks away in disbelief ...
I got talent that nobody knows about
That sort of makes me like God, right?

Say man, get your throat off that gun

It's in the way you talk, man

This liquor store is a has been
But I got new followers
I got new ideas, man
I'm gonna put some history on this canvas
I'm gonna put some things on your mind ... like God

I'm not going to sleep for twenty years

My son is across the street
I'm going to talk to him
I'm going to tell him something he's never heard
I'm going to teach him how to make a dollar
know better than to say anything back.
Like God

I might never sleep again

I've rolled it all into one

This is my part

Who did you kill?
... You making my afterlife boring, man

Nobody's across the street now ... look ... nobody's there now

Talent ... tell me something ... tell me about that trumpet walk to
God

I know you can't ...
I know you

You can't offend me. I'm just getting started

3. The Sermon

I guess we're all city people now
And we roam around carving "still alive" in people's foreheads
(preaching gently)

How do you find our city?
Lovely coliseums your trash piles make

Hate like this pushes people to speed . . .
Makes it romantic for armed robbery and talkative friends

    Makes you go off to whisper at a wall
        Because everybody is there in that wall
          And they are not coming back
            They are poor
                We are wretched
                We are a few hundred hands

A few hundred voices
Talking to a prophet that someone made up.
Would you like us to make you up a prophet?
Would you like us to pretend that you're not home
That you're not poor
We hope you got some aggression in that cup
We hope you dig this prophet we've made you
Sincerely we do
Dig our invincibility
Object made intention

Made animated
Made religion
Made drug
Like a switchblade weeping in the back of a two-viewer wake
Like on the table is everything you ever loved
Take a trembling bite
No, binge
On objects made legends
Like the knife you bought your sister
The shotgun seat you swear someone is always riding in
Black Hands
not the Black Hands they fantasize about,
No, the Black Hands that are never left out when it is time to
    save our lives

Hangman,
There will be no third person this morning
The sky won't stay the same color
And traffic features 144,000 nervous musicians
Best time to be born is today
Like going outside and coming right back in the house
Best time to be high too
Like going in the house and coming right back outside

    And they might shoot you through an exit
        for the sake of telling a funnier story
            People are newspapers
            and actors
            And the congregation is all going to die in character

4. When the Sermon Ends

Pace yourself, junkie
That's not a pedal
Nor floor
That's a heart rate
with a sense of humor
That's a muffled twin too smothered
to be evil
That's someone who needs you on the phone

relax, junkie
The night isn't one big ghost only obsessed
with your kitchen
The night got nothing to do with you

Look at you,
in a family-less portrait painted to some funk
somewhere in the gutter
undecidedly titled, "Run"

Look at you,
you don't know what to smile about next
you don't know what's in the refrigerator
you don't know what your father should have told you
back when you were an angry baby

things like
"revenge is for movies"

or
"don't worry about paying rent,
worry about how many people
fear your name"
good scholarship like
"monarchy exists in gas stations"
"the color of dope is gold"
"make a name for yourself while
there are still people around here
who pray for you"

nightmares written under your fingernails
after a dig through your chest

suicide is nothing but some word close to culture
don't worry
this is the page that nobody's paying attention to

last-minute heroin breaks
between new friends
public bus friends
so and so is your so and so friends
go meet the easygoing side door
with a funny story and all the money
here's your half of the river
stay as long as nobody calls
hold your own head
but don't be nervous
around here we all get sleepy at the same time

stretching a mask is easy to master
lean away from breath
into panic
into the blindside
you're three angles away from a house
with better money under the mattress

5. Under the Aftermath

You ever sat on the couch while your body was at the window, hands and forehead pressed against the glass? And wondered what that feeling in your chest had to do with the groceries. And what her smile had to do with the light bill. And where the couch came from. Who else had or had not escaped it. And you are not going anywhere. There is uneven time in the angles of this room. Slave catchers' fingernails and fingerless prayers. The narrators in this room mean to tell of your downfall. Fingerless prayers for that too. Everything thinks it is a thief born heroically empty. Life is just another bedroom split. A bunch of deadly things that feel sorry for themselves. And sorry, you are not that deadly.

You know, whispers work backwards too
And claim no king
Lower your eyes onto this neighborhood individualism
And let this individualism read you too

Take one last self-portrait with you on your way to the floor
You got quiet brothers all over this room
We won't break your fall
We won't wake you up
But while you sleep

Nothing will touch you
6. *When the Aftermath Ends*

I let a stray dog into my house

He looked at the ceiling and told me his dream of new pennies

I asked am I being took

He said,
"No. These pennies mean we are in water."

I said, fountain?
Then asked, river?

He said,
"You are stray too"

A tale of no city
Where a bloodstain has no beginning
A heart attack has no end
A gun for a keeper
A street sign for a friend
And dead men don't know any other tales
Other than the one where the world goes away

Empty spaces

I been thinking about this picture I want to draw

It's going to have vacant hands
Still feared

It's gonna have pain with empty spaces

                                        Tools that choose us

It's gonna have catchy violence

                            Someone will be poor and alone

African born

                    There will be the way

The gathering   The gun handle

                                        The palm where the gun
                                            feels protected
                                              then speaks

Empty space

        An un-played build

More hands
                Purple

                Grey scent that can be seen

                                                        Me
                                                In no more

Implied piano
        In tilted heads

Top right corner
There's going to be a red figure

Yellowing space

                        An ancient woman
                    presented in four faces

                                        Street sign maybe
                                        Street light maybe

An ancient man
presented in shoulders

It's going to have the woman I love

Lower left corner
A blue horn

Yellowing space

                                                No moon

A gangster maybe

Eyes that are earlier than comprehension

To these eyes
Love is sacred
But only a baby

To these eyes
All of the rest drifts

Brown with veins

Black with fingers

Empty space

Eyes
Presented in generations

Ceiling Traffic

I walked off the plane somewhere over Ohio

a gesture that meant a lot to worshipers in border churches
(and schoolchildren restless enough to write short stories on their
sleeves)

the distance between my keys and my money
has to be the punchline in a joke about a good day

I know everything in the world except how to get to the back stairs

... At least eventually

I've fallen asleep on the floor for the first time in Baltimore

And my career as a criminal ends anticlimactically
but formally ... and buried in art

"When you lay down where a murder took place, pray that
everybody took the long way home ... for one time in your life,
don't look over your shoulder ... don't go choking yourself on
passengers' purse straps"
                    —advice ignored with all the rest of five minutes ago

I woke up
Just one more in a pair of scabs
On an ark of scabs
        is the mattress in on my ransom?

is that shade I enjoy in the color red?
           —depends on what I've been calling myself lately

One shot
      then noon has a candle

I've never seen so many names reduced to detail with the firing
    of one shot

*Nothing on her mind about me. Or so this strange lake tells me. I
don't know what love is. But this I am sure is a lake. What window
am I supposed to stare out of if nowhere will let me in?*
           —working class windows is all my cigarette knows

Blown off in the middle of the night
I guess it is still the next morning

                  Me and my friend laugh
                       She laughs harder

Then I rolled over half drunk in my shotgun seat

And all the almost famous people fall down
And I will fall asleep over this page five times before it's all said
    and done
And five times will have no significance by the time it's all said
    and done

And can't say I had completely wasted my time
Being shaken down for two dollars by parking lot security

Makes for a good deathbed flashback

And I wasted a reputation that nobody in this town cares about
                           —Some welcomed significance

Imagine a summer of these kinds of relationships
And the art this was five minutes ago

                    I move a pawn against an empty chair

                              That is the courage

May Day

under the house, but treated well by the 1970s

A class struggle
        sacred and soon

while we spend the new sea level at the store with morbid people
who sell alcohol and alcohol for the man

                                This morning is a zoo in love
                                A killing field's smile

Where they send applause in front of their troops,

                                "We got plenty of pain
                                    to stay on this guitar
                                    for one hundred years"

When a neighborhood is in pain, houses stutter at each other
In a theater of human and plaster

No one ever goes free, but the walls become more thoughtful and
remember our names

Men think they are passing around cigarettes
But really cigarettes are passing around men

                                houses stutter at each other
                                about the rich man's world

                              and the poor man's water
                              about the rich man's world
                              and the poor man's repetition

Ex-workers have hunched shoulders that fit between stairs and
    headaches / An inverted purgatory / Of course their children
    feel at home everywhere

Hands slur as they speak
            a man is lamppost high
            Is his lamppost's keeper

                              the alarms are paved with gold

"futureless is this music and this music's proprietors"

                        Children make better skylines out of wino's tales
            And it takes one (lamppost high … his lamppost's keeper)

Incarcerated children next to the lightning
Across the jar from purgatory

                              Happy just to see something in motion,
                        We welcome the north american drumroll

    A moth flies to the right of this definition of north america

    A moth flies to the right of twenty-five floors of brick astronomy

Europe rises to our 25th-floor window

Carrying headaches and mirrors

We should close the window
But we haven't finished our cigarettes

"the alarm is paved with gold,"
the morbid person declares
while grinning and crying

                "you are going to get
            the gun under the counter wet,"

                              we warn as we only grin

Pointing At Passengers

his eyes were a realm to the right.

this picture is rushed
his eyes were rushing   a red simple

we are young. death is even younger
and clumsy ... bumping into our crowd   a hungry simple

this street is disturbed and informal and bored out of its animation

San Francisco will kill you

> I'm bad with faces
> and have dreamed of millions
> I am small
> and owe everybody in this projection
> more personality

... when no one was lying, no matter what lies had brought us
there ... to end. windows to intentions and me. near to God.
where gravity finds its transition and the second-to-last meal for
my senses. grey cascading behind a pistol. a hand extending from
a horizon size slide. then we waited because we were sincere.
someone intervened. forget her name. near to God. when all these
faces. windows to intentions. when all of this world / went to the
ground.

Rough feeling now
rushing down
a two-lane ravine

Get in
And don't get killed

Rushing now
She knew I wasn't eating
Lightning does not count as a meal
Nor as a dream

Please sleep

She has saved me a plate
She listens only because she likes me

—Lightning ends

remove my heart racing, and babylon is fine

go ahead and call these hours daytime /
we will rip the light off the walls

booster sings the blues
ten feet from the escalator

I clap for her set
with yellow teeth

"the first 50 hours of resurrection are beautiful,"
says the man holding the door

I give him a dollar
50 for me
50 for her

mention seasons to the three of us
if you want to see dragons laugh

Many Doses To Go
or
Turns the Pen

Coal mine comedian:

> Laugh
> Die a little
> Laugh

His feet up on some table
they used to sacrifice friendly people on
"feet first this time," I laugh when he says

"I'll be driving out of town for the next five minutes"
—how we relate to our modern posture

"I'll take a room with a view of the alley, please"
"I will turn half the TV on"
"I've been human too long tonight ... and it's barely tonight."
"Sipping from this bottle I've taken to calling a borrowed book"

He writes free like ... friendless like
"I know what I am doing," said his character
"I know what I am doing," repeated the writer
"This fight might help," said his character
"This fight might help," lied the writer

writing about the twigs of modern nationalism

the country goes away first ... then third

barracks and precincts de-people

a country dismantled with syringes (even tweezers)

a poorly narrated knife toss (and theory)
—neither curse nor trophy

New York City banister
singing some funk /
the man sings down the stairs
silent when he opens the trunk

"I clean up well and will be the only person in heaven"

on the diabolically grown side of town
watching people and hanging onto every shift in weight
he likes the concept of fathers
his hands make good city mortar
wondering when remorse will wear off
wondering who sent that basket of rats

he's forgot what world he's parallel to

the barcode got good to him

"Underwater is where I say I grew up
when I have run out of things to say"

Wit got us dinner
Or so the last conversation

Was supposed to keep us alive
"I wasn't always in heaven like this"

"Man, you are a city-less light show ... a bargain shopper in Paris"

A story that everyone's been

Falling backwards doing 70 mph
I can feel rubble washing over my shoulders

I will be August cloth and the absence of a real friend

   —If this fog is clapping for you, I might as well, too—

                  A young woman sings a fugitive set list
She sings, "poetry is a mother's pain … as are most things avenged."
   She sings, "jail guards only pray when the governor is looking."

                        All underworld approval is a loan
                              In a pacific state
                        Card table under poems
                        Also inching through a forearm

back alley arguments and the
veterans who forgot they had them
through downtown canyons
              calming predawn dogs
                     I mean this city sleeps

We are stretched out on falling stained glass
Or written in scraps
Or a story about a whisky child
And the river talks in the end

Settled like hips under a smaller hand under his

Child of God smokes his third cigarette in the kitchen
Bloodline somewhere near the drain

He didn't stick around

A few winters' worth of house keys
And nine dollars on the night table

I love her still

And what's not to love
New jokes at 10am are not easy to pull off

At 10am I thought of oppression

Found an unlikely appetite in a bus station
Next to a man's forfeited cigarette drags

"These shoes didn't leave the house clean.
Why should I care now?"

Four Walls

A lot of God can happen in three seconds
                              Not much heaven though

Here is a man before a fight: A leave-me-alone type of character
emerging from the penniless death
of a one-way-street fiction
                    I mean I'm going to make it
                    even if I have to drive backwards

All I have is chord changes and a thousand backhands
                    Driving a street like I'm choking it

                                        Car full of nephews
                              There hasn't been a son since November
                  And there hasn't been a street I can't choke to death

                                        This city better back down

See this gun on the table
And something about staring until it all feels stable

                              Why wouldn't I protect everyone

                              All my deaths sleep late
                              And I name them all

My son better be quick
My daughter better shoot first

Because we fold for no one
We fold for nothing

Ok, the first thing you'll feel is a heat
       This lady would tell me
        Telling me about possession
Drink life neat is what I'd mostly hear
And most of the world leaves me alone

             To breathe smog like a giant
          To go to jail every once in a while

When the genocide kicks up in late May
When politicians have too easy a time:

               I'm gassing backwards out of a one-way street
                   In honor of myself
And in honor of you (if you understand the nature of the world)

                      How long have I been
                      just like my father
                      One hell of a
                      resemblance says the
                      anxiety of five men
                      This is crossroads
                      Crossroads narrative
                      So much crossroad that
                      they got in the habit of
                      turning back
                      Turn back only to

find themselves
remembering me
But not my last words
A man before a fight

You will feel a heat
But there's nothing to keep in mind
Nothing to remember
Really nothing to be
Just this moment
Then another
Then stare
Then it all becomes stable
Then the table legs go fuzzy
And Friday is an unfamiliar face peeking through the window

It's cool to panic for a second
Composure is wasted on your worst enemies

    People are marked on that sidewalk
    You are the only thing life-sized
    Everybody knows this
    In a wire hanger empire
    When the blood stops walking
    This feeling isn't father enough to be permission to fold
    You better swing one more time

That father of yours
Rose from the grave and said, just give me five more minutes

Said, running water is a myth
It's us who run up, down, and along the side of this water

And people don't rise from the grave
They are not laid down neither
It's us who flip all round their body

So beware when the people around you look like they are about to jump
It might be your time

You'll feel a heat

And when four walls demand to be four walls
And the earth outside mutes
Do not panic

Do not recreate the earth outside
Do not tell jokes to yourself
Do not talk disrespectfully to the four walls
Instead, unclench your fist and walk away

There might be heaven
If you understand the nature of the world

Scenes Do Not Flee

"Make it about love. And make it predictable."

I promise that I have a real live girlfriend
We are going to drive to Mexico tomorrow
I will be riding in the trunk

I'm in a real live relationship
Dancing up the steps (old school)
On the way to Mexico
Riding on the roof
Dancing there too

Making the time stretch
I've made it to the back seat,
But got nothing to say

I've made it to the wheel,
But now it's time to go home

Three buildings make a tide

I do not regret the things I said to that wall
stories about hand ratios in brawls
and a hotel kitchen entrance killer
and steamboats where they dedicate their one-night stand to
    driftwood
                While we look at all the pretty kingdoms floating
                   over our tents
                       While we get the surplus treatment

Don't put your shoe on my shoulder
And call it a hand (one building makes a jail)

"that's a lot of people for
only a little bit of commotion"

                      The bookshelf looks alive to me
        Alive and my opposition (until the devil lets me go)

                My sidekick is the bootlegger

I tied up our friend as soon as a couple rich people acted like they
                      cared about him

            A painting of a sun watched me end lives

The point I was making began scaring other patrons in the pool hall

"who would name themselves after this city?"
—to which I reply, "the only woman for me."

Calling my drug the scoundrel and cousin / an axe handle in its
    five minutes as a twin

Painting my walls with pieces of other walls

                  I wandered to the edge of the parking lot

A stranger is a stranger

Half-eaten canvas frames
we are allowed
to survive by
mid-level riffs

Loved you ...
      not the jungle

Customer abandonment ...
      other than more family

Look back at me, people ...
In Chicago with Appalachian piety

In cuffs, wishing I was more drunk ...
the beginning of the end of the world ... all worlds

The gun gets personified then impressed

The universe has themes   Like being mute in a dream
Like secondhand polaroid pictures   Like reminding family of your
father

Like old friends we catch up awkwardly
    A forgettable blues
        He's four cigarettes into his thoughts

to live with fear
is all everyone does downstairs

up here
there's something much worse

Tripwire eyes
      We are both men passing out
            We are both comfortable, but for opposite reasons

Puppets Where You Found Them

The city loves me back now
—It was him or me

A shortcut through your girlfriend's apartment
landed me into three inside jokes and (and about) a headache.
I break every watch my friends wear while they follow the red queen.
I once had a happy four months walking to my car with nervous tics
    and no gun.
I don't mean to talk fast. Just got a lot of soul to get off my chest (souls,
    too).

                    Good for you, I thought about the man
                    Then returned to cursing

I suppose drugs don't last longer
Back alley in a back neighborhood
Where someone always goes to work drunk
And hard as they pray
The car always starts

                    Talking to you from a window
                    Five blocks away
                    Room full of
                    Black Art
                    Black Communism
                    And pictures of you all

Conquered house wood / Then the cops come

Walk through this cold sweat
Until the remorse wears off
or
Run the pint back to the store
and shoot the sign down

reading good books about revenge:

Sometimes I am a king

My car is different around the corner

I must be a child
Because I haven't eaten

Done then undone exists the peace

You don't want to die playing here
Before a packed, disinterested house
Lack of higher ground
Brown boat in a blood stream
Waves do everything except rewind

And So My Strength

Soft and shoulder and soon
The world is now careful and few

Nobody's son is in this story
A man exits an everywhere for you

Raspy brief lives I enter with hands full of his memories

Remember that dusk?
I like that dusk
The way we untie the blue

Again

Again man exits
He has gambler hands
Gambler hands that only know you
Untie blue
In my only home

I need a lounge all wood
        A bar on planks with chain gang lights
I need my last burning double
        My father's son on guitar
Sweating trees   Clean shoes   Somebody in red
                Teeth in smoke   Red smoke with personality

Steam owning the windows in front of two kids who now can't see

More smoky teeth   Renaissance composed faces

My father's son with a genius right hand

—All in the 5 seconds her eyes are only on me

                        Guitar strings

               Can you see his guitar strings?
        Stretched from day one to a numb dirt
          They say that man was music first

        They say give your loved ones a grave to visit
None of us are children behind this ancient green face
                  —type of religion

He calls the sky an acquaintance for the sake of that ring / Guitar
    strings from grandfather to grandson / Smokestack chapter /
    Strum to his heart's confusion / Acquaintances tip hats / Now
    where's the sky?

Where's the pain from last night?
—type of chord change

where's my lady?
—type of corner pocket shot

guitar strings from shot glass to bar top

                   that one he wrote for his lady

                                        as suggested by the sky
                                            —type of night

nice voice for listening
for one who listens to me
—type of thing the sky would say

guitar strings between me and you / acquaintances along the
    way / part ways to our lyrics / until the dirt tastes some of this
    troublesome / and I can finally hear the shot glass sky / smoke
    bath resurrection / then guitar strings / then her belly / then
    guitar strings / then last night

in case sketches don't return me
it was always you

sea salt and me   see a tide stand still   then become a crashing soil

see a bed . . .
flying and alive

then a red charcoal me   fire that isn't blind   at my best

see a witness stand still   window introduction again in
                                      charcoal lines

the same breeze your hand remembers   a breeze that isn't blind

sea salt and me   an ocean burning low   words on a forearm

                                98

two shadows in freedom   windowsill commitment

see me again   saw me before   deeply

All Bets

If only you had talked heroically to yourself too

    Then maybe your closest friends would have survived the shelter
                (And the feds and artisans that put us there)

I would like to tell you that somewhere
Despite the checkpoints
There is an apostle body in which I can be free

Riding the bus watching arms falling off
is a pastime in the minimum-security quarters

                    Post-proletariat mothers
                    Make coming outside
        Worth being followed through the low end

Oh, but this project lobby does host an art gallery between uprisings

"I thought you kept an american rug under your feet … I mean if
    you want your army to grow."

I can't tell you about myself and something backwards coming up
    through the page at the same time

like water switching places with you, nuclear populism, and
five-dollar greed

The next-door stalemate
But we are going to keep hero worship out of this story
And it was all cool when the weather was worse

Something about the worst society to write a poem in

Something about the last laugh a baby has
Before he cries for the rest of his life
—a poem before streets start

"you are a cold blooded criminal … you just don't mean to be"

Going to be the Poor Man's Star

I smoked my first joint today
I will not remember with whom
I will not remember the monkhood of being high
I will not have a year to brag about

I took that year farther today
I was the only one there
I will not have a year to brag about to the wrong person
I will have a night
And then one more day

Blacksmith plays the piano
  And the good life begs me all night for a definition

I'm in a dream. A spirit world. You should introduce yourself. And
  convince me to sleep.

    my wallet   jumped over the book
my wallet   jumped over the desert

    None of us ate good for three days
    Maybe someone woke up in jail
    or woke up outside furious for a decade
    author of a grudge kite or sudden religion

I'll be your grandfather
If myself or a grandfather will lead you to your power
—a music lesson

They all crouch behind me ... and why shouldn't Harlem
kill

                                        for its musicians

You are a star, I bet

Where it's too warm to be a trench
But I'm too tired to be a civilian

the penny smell on the ceiling
                and the condition of our hands
                show how the real nightlife out here
                is an expanding dream of threes

                in which characters cut off their ring fingers
                and wave at the ground

Conscience hurt my chances ...
        broke into my shoulder blade ...
                picture me: walking to some money under my breath

So He Sings Along

Sweet hands around my throat ... hands that I don't really feel
—the drummer struggles

the soul between a soul and the bus window ...
it's not a life
it's an emotion
that also mumbles
in a room of material
because everything
is parallel to a mumble

Breathing real paint
Burning down a real world

Channels to fall asleep to

While shoebox to shoebox travels my childhood

Professionals roll garbage cans around a conference room
Half the size of a holding tank
Half the hope of a holding tank
Full of third world retail flattery
"nothing wrong with the blind leading the blind,"
                                        we think they just said

porcelain epoch
succeeding for the most part
dying for the most part
married for the most part to its death

when a hostage has a hostage
that is u.s. education

stores detach their heads
and expect you to do the same when you enter

God says, "do not trust me in this room"

Two fascists walk into a bar
One says, "let's make a baby."
The other says, "let's make three … and let the first one eat the
other two."

                              your sky or mine
                                read from
                    the book of poolroom enemies

"I'm the best kind of square. Poor and in love with the 1960s.
          The first picture I ever saw in my life faded
                from my storytelling a long time ago."

Not even ten years old
And most of you are on my shoulders

The store's detached head smiled

casually be poor
          teach yourself
          how to get out of this room
          and we'll leave you enough blood
          to turn off the lights on your way out

casually be poor ...
          they are all cops when you are poor

For My Best Friend

We are losing the intensive care unit waiting room war

We were doing so well
        So well we got sleepy
                So sleepy the institution returned

In the 8th adjoined room sleeping on the 8th adjoined chair

The last five minutes just like the first

Hands behind teeth / teeth behind us

Wall plans decorated with her favorite mannerisms

Flight / within a subtle sweep

Or institution light leaps off of a dreamt thought
                                        ... in time

                                    She saved my life before,
                                            you know,
                                all of them ... those lives
                                                    mine
One way or the other, every story is told backwards or twice

And waking up rough is the same as going roughly into a dream
—is also something her eyes would say

Your sister is not going home

Cut a Hand From a Hand

"if you reverse the car any farther,
you will run over all the scenes in the back of your mind"

I never cared for teachers ... just the pattern of their fainting spells
      induced by wall art
Propaganda is courage, man

The price sticker hides my tattoo
—I treasure my problem with the world

"My mother becomes from Brooklyn first thing in the morning"
—a proverb around these parts
            proverb or peasant entrance password

Writing short notes to famous Europeans
On the backs of post cards
With ransom requests

They reply with a newsreel or cigarette announcement (I can't tell
      the difference)

                              Noble dollars then you die inside
                                    (but only inside)

"They call it, 'sleeping deeper than your stalker.'
And stalker is all that badge makes you,"
says a great spirit dressed in the
bloody rags tuxedos became

Meanwhile my punch is feared by no one
"Proud of yourself?" I ask the fret hand

"Porch Lights" is what they call our guns

I've seen this house in a dream

I believe a trumpet was the first possessed object to fly

"keep going," she cheers

the draft in the room becomes a toddler
toddler obsessed with the altar
the altar becomes a runaway train

got a thousand paintings cascading down my skinny arms
dictionaries piling up to the window bars

—a reminder to the population that
your blanket can work with
or against you—
human reef /
we will be a big human reef
for concepts that finally gain a metaphysical nature
and they will swim around our beautiful poses

we stop being flashbacks
then stop being three different people
then I was alone [the pistol is one city away]

one of the drug triangle's lines runs through my head
I tap the bottle twice and consider the dead refreshed
"don't you want to rest your bravery?
don't you want to be a coward for a little bit?"
—back and forth to a panic attack with no problems nor fears

a man gets a facial expression finally
a Friday finally goes his way
his life is finally talked about happily in his head

I can't possess the body of a hermit
I must be the last of his smoke
Now running away with three blocks of alley
Tucked under my arm
You ever see a man
get to the bottom of his soul
in a car ride down a missing cousin's street?

Half step to the right
I mean I took the whole car outside of history
Half step to the right
I mean a whole pack of wolves stepped to my left

"road marker" is what I called the light bulb we had for a sun
a whole civilization might slink to the sink
chain gang shuffling next to a sucker

—the long look in the mirror [a stack of money starts talking
from four cities away]

Three Nights In A Row

The floorboards were right where
the bottle said they would be

you should be good at this by now

the lights went off
and all the funeral programs came to life

the dealer's seat is empty
as my heart fusses
writing poems before they come to pass

or I've been sitting
in an inner-city park for too long

I write rhymes between sips
I write sips too
one-man nationalism
cut all bones
and then teeth

or I'm not the one who wrote this down

I dipped my thumb into the vortex
and went wherever
I was told reparations was

metal worker you might as well call me

Fragile city
I got a disagreement
with everyone north of Geary Street
I know what happens
next to my bummiest friends

the line between good art and a good car chase
finally became thin this year
the price of good art becomes a car chase next year

burn those crops for them, timid city
then the post slavery slot machines next

pass me that picture of your family

the view
sees you

or a group of friends
can stop pretending
like they are not
just one person
staring at a box of cigarettes

But Rooftops Did All the Work

Half asleep was my tutor
When I played my hand violently for the first time

"I'm snorting cocaine on the back of a poorly decorated camel,"
I told the choir as they rushed out of the church doors

"why are you all running in a drought?"

    I wasn't drunk when I said things to scare and / or mock people
                        I am a mock person
                           Clocks where the toilet
                apparently does not need to be anymore

"at least I know where my veins are metaphors."
—talking about facts that
the choir will never be able to handle

(they are somewhere pretending that they are in the desert)

"my veins are metaphors right here, chumps!"

                                 "it wasn't my idea,"
                      I say watching the library burn

"Go ahead now. Run to the corner store
and let the oligarchy know that everything is alright"

people / walking confidently down the street with their real
    arms reaching up

people / walking confidently down the street
            walking on top of their real clothes

people / naked with their hands up

                              man, heaven sure is secretive

                         The staircase under this slavery
                         And one hundred slaves

For a delicate five dollars
I made a deal early in life
But now I feel like hanging in there a little longer
        —when human flight becomes the fall that nobody saw

I am influenced by it all
—as is the custom

I do not trust immortal people
And therefore hope to not become one

"I'm a bluesman. Of course I mean to kill you."

                    You look like an occasionally violent man
                            not in charge of an altar
                not in charge of an important altar, anyway
                    not one that is about fancy deities

just a plain neighborhood for the dead

please give me
spare change and your word that I won't be missing in a year

 —as is the custom, two humans make a humanity

I Almost Go Away

Sorry I'm late, dear
But I do not know you anymore

My back against the seat as I walk to her apartment

My back against the seat as I walk up her steps

My back against the seat as the apartment isn't there

> She waits in the hospital lobby
> With twenty voices behind her fingers

>> "but I can now fly," she says
>> and they agree

I am a proletariat-folding-chair class victim
Surrounded by the color you only see on folding chairs

You know me now

> I should have never lived the last two days
> The way I did

>> Faceless down in a puddle
>> In a collage of puddles

And we feel that after sinking
We will still be on top of the world

A Black world, baby

Did you see heaven just move a mile higher out of jealousy
And the air start talking to itself
All to the detriment of everyone else in this city

11pm conversation and she has already woken up the next
morning

                              on a street that would rather be a ceiling

                                        the scramble of our hands
                                        playing "where is the grin"

hey, whether I trip over everything on the avenue or not
getting there is getting there
so drink up and stop looking away

kick the river all night if you want

something about the reinvention of street life
and the inside jokes between a scared kid and a cutter
in a room that is sort of about rites

we never see each other again
especially not in other people

Fish With Ambition to Become the River

I looked in my bank account

It said, "You have five toilets to your name."
It said, "Don't just sit there. Return fire."

Talking head says, "Go to sleep children. You will all be police
    tomorrow."

We say: No. We will be the poor.

Talking head says, "Ok scumbags, I talked to you like children;
    now you will be dogs."

"Market Street" is the best two-word joke I have ever heard in
    San Francisco

"Now I have to teach myself how to pass out sketches and throw
    pencils at pigeons when I retire"

"I don't have any friends who would reprimand me anyway"
"Retire to the ocean and walk backwards into the surf
            pretending to fight off the weirdly dressed hordes"

                    —and I used to joke about being underwater.

Laughed at the people stealing my cigarettes
Laughed at the people pretending to tie my shoes

"now I have to put charcoal under the classroom and do
   impossible things with tap water"

"leave the window open so that the most respectful rats will come
   in and white enlightenment will have something to ponder."

—oh, what machines may come

"I should have never quit heroin," we all say (all of the time)

we started early
twenty wagons appeared in a dream I had about the 7th grade

Pathology needs a god to represent it to children and childlike states

Eat your people today

The top of the tornado starts under the soles of our shoes
And touches down on prison farms
Bibles offer no explanation
But one cool preacher has quite a laugh

All looked up at our beautiful shoes

                              "You still keep that knife in the car."
                                   —the reality is
                                   that I am awake
                                   and listening to an
                                   argument outside

half listening
half fighting alongside

—the reality is
that I am built
to protect religion
but not all of the time

"I was watching her on my hands"
"even my imagination just sat there"

"the entire crowd did not take a sip for twenty minutes"

—the choir is done with you
done with all of us

"We call those projects 'The Jar'"
the private said to himself
while working on his birthday

"backflip and become a man"
we said as we aimed

"lie down right over there.
We hid the beds behind the trash"

—the rest of the crash course came in the morning

"like you've never seen this card trick before
the one where your grandfather appears

and throws a couple of people into a fire"
—just let it rockslide into that shot glass

I should have talked to her

instead I threw my whole life away

I turned my back on my people, Lord

left them for a trip up three flights of stairs

now the whole freak show is on the back of my hand

including capitalists looking up at the sky

what fascists are determined to do
does not scare most people

it makes most people bored
but we want our grandparents to survive ...

Dear grandfather,

I met some bluesmen today.
Vanquished them all.
I declared, "your lady is with you,
but all these chairs in here
are mine."

Before I opened the door to the street
      I knocked
                And the world let me in

Stumbled outside
And there were miles and miles
Of chalk outlines and window curtains
littered across the earth's city

                                        Dear Bluesmen,

                        Now I am deader than you.
                              Please take your seats.
                              —the title of our song

The Oldest Then The Youngest

Grandmother, why don't you ever talk about your children who
the first world murdered?

Because, son, I haven't run out of knife handles.
Hang this one around your neck so that your brothers and sisters
will know what you are

The first white man invented the first flagpole
while inspired by the first hole he ever put in a human being

I don't count in your story
There's no face on your coin

Here come the horns out of the water

I've never seen
I mean I've never looked at the handcuffs on my wrist
And wondered how rusted yours must be by now
—See you around—

There goes the mob into the water / I lie, but not all the time

No throat. Our enemy has no throat, Grandmother
What joker then did I hear scream a museum of laughter at us
    all night?

Rusted by now
—You are the one-legged human blackbird—

You want me to haunt the road, Grandmother?
Make them lay blessed and cursed coins on guard rails

me personally, I like dying for nothing

returning in a methodically decorated revenge mask

fingernails only good for counting days in basement stone

Grandmother, my brothers knew me right away / They warned me
    that my ribcage would be the linchpin of all industry /
    Suddenly I saw every soldier that ever lived and would live
    punch in / I saw a white man sketching the meat hooks into
    my angled carcass / And little white children danced tunnels
    out of my side / Look what your ribs have become

my brothers told me I was the deathwish child

with patches from all masks on mine

—two sides to one personality, you know
the friend who is friend
to things you cannot see
lazy things
where you are the water
and the river walks around
where you are the water
and the ocean holds no souls—

too many more nights like this
and they will forget my name
like minded
were our fathers

in rooms full of neck wounds
I will be king
Walking around kicking out chairs
The head of the basement church
Clock hands trembling on behalf of a handcuffed congregation

Cushy employment
You would call dying young

Happy just to no longer be the baby that crawled alone

Crawled alone on a carpet
        Carpet in the alley

Every citizen
Sort of watching
Eyes under their breath

Four buses coming at a time
Not picking up or dropping off one wise man

Here come the horns out the water
Horn players not too far behind
Here come the protest signs
Here comes the chorus

A spirit shape in the gutter trash
—their art lies about us
the contest was for the last book to ever be burned—

The whole room cried to itself
Then I controlled the room
For a little while
(because that is all I could think to do)

—we put a napkin over the blood and a red desert appeared
what have we soaked ourselves into?
the desert then spit up an intersection
and I was a lamppost poster about revolution
we are children who are friends with children who have wings
fixated on first-floor window bars designed for Europeans
(one out of the only two designs in the world)—

I wrote rhymes for my people

They all ended well

Found my mask on a 1968 shotgun seat

I added a patch while wearing it on my face
Using the side-view mirror

It was a long night for my friends

Driving around the city
Helping me kick out chairs

The city
Closing down sideways
Like buildings half-turned to run back to the wilderness
(religious half measures)

*The first time I dangled, blackbirds told me they would not be
my friends*

*I held on
Somewhere in me godlike
Or gold wall for a people's belief*

*Don't bow, cousins
Watch me a little, then go fight*

The second time I dangled, the blackbirds looked bored

*They shuffled on overcrowded branches making small talk about
stories they thought were pathetic*

*Bow, cousins
—the third time I dangle*

The world was passing your killer by, my friend
He still doesn't see himself in you

He never exactly did the crime
He didn't see himself in much, my friend
In a chair he doesn't want to use
He listens to his associates joke

The ceiling and I
are alone

among other things we brag about
having in common

I am homeless again

Let me borrow your blackbirds

Show them around the city

Show them the alley carpets

And everywhere else I cut out a patch for my mask

Discount bedding and county jail sweatpants
I got a Bible page over my scalp

A chapter to spite protest signs

The best the dead can do is let me play doorman

Grandmother, now we are all friends

I brought them the knife handle

They walk me wherever I need to go
—these blackbirds

                                    I am safely home
                                    And our houses
                                    Are on a freight train

"I'm 18 feet under a country"

"walking upside down
where words work backwards against our good time
me and these cheap chess pieces
working against their own king
leave me to my TV static
leave me to sit at the bottom of a river full of barbed-wire spikes
    and plastic grain"

TV static the way I breathe before the first look at the door in the
morning. You tough outside, but can't look the spoon in the eye
right now. What godhood had me first? Does my nature watch
over or scatter the pictures in living rooms? Have I rested my hand
on everything except people?

"my hand sign to God, you better leave me to my peace
I mean stop calling every damn thing a whirlwind
let me borrow your blackbirds, too
leave me alone"

a song that is plenty empty
so many characters missing from it, genocide can't be prosecuted
    correctly
a nightmare that is plenty void
a chorus's confusion

Grandmother, I will check on all your children

Don't Take Care of Yourself, Son

Take Care of This Knife Handle

do not bow, cousins

watch me a little longer

"I believe I am a twin"

"I hear he has never been taken alive"

"when I shuffle postcards
discolored months
fold into each other"

"the seasons flicker through my hands"

"sun and everything else that impresses older versions of myself"

"ease into this slave ship with me"

"nothing will be over for a really long time"

"ease into this side bet about a Bible story
and everything else that impresses younger versions of myself"

"Grandmother, I will write them after I eat"

                              I believe that I am a twin
                                My brain is not mine
                                More like mine again

Just like everything else in this life

—We put a delicate five dollars on the table
And all the souls in the room rejoiced
We are cheap people and therefore always gambling
World history has a proletariat when the lights come back on—

                              I don't know if I got a soul
                                If I can't have a city

Warlords, run

I'm going back to a gold wall

I'm going back to a bind
Blind under my breath

"cheap chess pieces and me next"

—some type of series of numbers and symbols
flows from the tap
and I liked me better small, too
liked the view
all the violence under various tables—

"there is a stomach in my stomach
set aside only for drugs"

there is a hand in my hand
set aside only for pieces of crumpled receipts
I wrote my first poem on
over and over

"the locals keep renaming this junkyard
it has one hundred decent nicknames
no one can name you better than the oppressed
I learned the new name, and in no time, became the most wanted"

"can't stand all this plastic my hand is made of"

I made the meal for the wolves
Then kept writing

I made the meal for a couple of cowards
Then kept on sleeping

Soul? That's what they say you got? Maybe you got a painting of
one folded up under that silly shirt. I'm famous in this living room.
I don't want to be famous anywhere else. Right here is perfect. It's
not prison.

—people mud up the street
until it's the rare skin
where we shuffled about
martyring godsons—

my head crawled into my chest
and a great sleep began

when you wake up
I will be three people

If I rumble, I will lose.

nation sort of collapses around the corner, brother / slippers to the
    factory bus on flats / fast taps on the dashboard, baby /
    ceremony then store

> *where you are the water*
> *and the rain eats too much*
> *and fights for no one*

I must really be the devil's front man. I must really be the hundred
musicians he has already talked to. "It's a simple matter," the devil
explains. "You give me all your lead. I give you all this gold. Then
one day, I return your lead." "What you then do with lead and
gold I leave to you," the devil says.

> doors and doors
> is all I ignore

watching people fold into each other
is a crying man's ritual

watching people make dear life out of their afternoons
is an evil man's ritual

"no hangman
ever really found confidence
drinking with others"
dissatisfied with the bullet
the storyteller started making sense
"paper bag clouds
and everyone is the rain"
improving fear / you may call it

—the man was slumped against a billboard
we wondered more about
how a billboard got to the ground
than the holes in his chest—

"leave the wounds and take the dreams"

—*they walk me wherever I want to go*

Tongo Eisen-Martin is the author of the critically acclaimed poetry book, *someone's dead already* (Bootstrap Press, 2015), and his poetry has been featured in *Harper's Magazine*. He is also a movement worker and educator whose work in Rikers Island was featured in the *New York Times*. He has been a faculty member at the Institute for Research in African-American Studies at Columbia University, and his curriculum on the extrajudicial killing of Black people, "We Charge Genocide Again!" has been used as an educational and organizing tool throughout the country.